Half Baked Harvest Cookbook

Half Baked Harvest Super Simple. Recipes for Instant, Overnight, Meal-Prepped, and Easy Comfort Foods

TABLE OF CONTENTS

BREAKFAST **10**

    GREEN VEGGIES QUICHE 10
    CHICKEN & ASPARAGUS FRITTATA 13
    SOUTHWEST SCRAMBLED EGG BITES 15
    BACON EGG BITES 17
    OMELET BITES 19
    CHEDDAR & BACON EGG BITES 21
    AVOCADO PICO EGG BITES 22
    BUTTERMILK GRIDDLE PANCAKES 24
    LEMONY PARMESAN BREADSTICKS 27

APPETIZER AND SIDES **29**

    COCONUT POTATOES 29
    SWEET POTATO AND WALNUTS MIX 31
    ROASTED SQUASH 32
    SQUASH PUREE 34
    WALNUT CAULIFLOWER RICE MIX 35

LUNCH **36**

    FIGS AND GOAT CHEESE-STUFFED CHICKEN 36
    CARNE ASADA 38
    AMAZING PULLED PORK 40
    BRAISED PORK BELLY 42

DINNER **43**

    LOW-CARB PORK MEDALLIONS 43
    ROSEMARY ROAST BEEF AND WHITE RADISHES 45
    BACON-WRAPPED PORK CHOPS 47
    ROSEMARY CHICKEN WITH AVOCADO SAUCE 48
    CRISPY CHICKEN NUGGETS 51
    ZUCCHINI & BELL PEPPER CHICKEN GRATIN 52
    COCONUT CHICKEN WITH CREAMY ASPARAGUS SAUCE ... 55
    HERB PORK CHOPS WITH CRANBERRY SAUCE 57
    PORK CHOPS WITH BASIL TOMATO SAUCE 59
    CITRUS PORK WITH SAUTÉED CABBAGE & TOMATOES 61

SOUP AND STEWS **63**

    CREAM OF BROCCOLI SOUP 63
    CHICKEN TORTILLA SOUP 65
    ITALIAN SAUSAGE AND POTATO SOUP 68
    BEEF AND BARLEY SOUP 70

Taco Soup 72

Chicken and Sausage Gumbo 73

VEGETABLES 75

Asian Vegetable Array with Quinoa Salad 75

Barely and Squash Salad 78

Grilled Veggies and Pasta Salad 80

Rustic Potato and Egg Salad 83

Roasted and Fresh Vegetable Salad 85

Strawberry, Almonds and Lettuce Salad 88

SNACK AND DESSERTS 90

Curry Spiced Almonds 90

Chia Peanut Butter Bites 91

Cheesy Sausage Dip 94

Salted Kale Chips 95

Bacon Jalapeno Quick Bread 97

Toasted Pumpkin Seeds 100

Bacon-Wrapped Burger Bites 102

Almond Sesame Crackers 103

Cauliflower Cheese Dip 105

Deviled Eggs with Bacon 107

BREAKFAST

Green Veggies Quiche

Preparation Time: 20 Minutes

Cooking Time: 20 Minutes

Servings: 4

Ingredients:

- Six organic eggs
- ½ cup unsweetened almond milk
- Salt and ground black pepper
- 2 cups baby spinach
- ½ cup green bell pepper
- One scallion
- ¼ cup cilantro
- One tablespoon chive,
- Three tablespoons mozzarella cheese

Directions:

1. Warm-up oven to 400ºF.

2. Grease a pie dish. Beat eggs, almond milk, salt, and black pepper. Set aside.
3. In another bowl, add the vegetables and herbs, then mix.
4. Place the veggie mixture and top with the egg mixture in the pie dish.
5. Bake within 20 minutes. Remove then sprinkle with the Parmesan cheese.
6. Slice and serve.

Nutrition: Calories 176 Net Carbs 4.1 g Total Fat 10.9 g Cholesterol 257 mg Protein 15.4 g

Chicken & Asparagus Frittata

Preparation Time: 15 Minutes

Cooking Time: 12 Minutes

Servings: 4

Ingredients:

- ½ cup grass-fed chicken breast
- 1/3 cup Parmesan cheese
- Six organic eggs
- Salt
- ground black pepper
- 1/3 cup boiled asparagus
- ¼ cup cherry tomatoes
- ¼ cup mozzarella cheese

Directions:

1. Warm-up broiler of the oven, then mix Parmesan cheese, eggs, salt, and black pepper in a bowl.
2. Melt butter, then cook the chicken and asparagus within 2–3 minutes.
3. Add the egg mixture and tomatoes and mix. Cook within 4–5 minutes.
4. Remove then sprinkle with the Parmesan cheese.

5. Transfer the wok under the broiler and broil within 3–4 minutes. Slice and serve.

Nutrition: Calories 158 Net Carbs 1.3 g Total Fat 9.3 g Cholesterol 265 mg

Southwest Scrambled Egg Bites

Preparation Time: 10 Minutes

Cooking Time: 23 Minutes

Servings: 4

Ingredients:

- Five eggs
- 1/2 teaspoon hot pepper sauce
- 1/3 cup tomatoes
- Three tablespoons green chilies
- One teaspoon black pepper
- 1/2 teaspoon salt
- Two tablespoons nondairy milk

Directions:

1. Mix both the eggs and milk in a large cup.
2. Add the hot sauce, pepper, and salt.
3. Put a small diced chilies and diced tomatoes in silicone cups. Fill each with 3/4 full with the egg mixture.
4. Put the trivet in the pot and pour 1 cup water. Put the mold on the trivet.
5. Set too high for 8 minutes. Cooldown before serving.

Nutrition: Calories: 106 Carbs: 2g Protein: 7.5g Fats: 7.4g

Bacon Egg Bites

Preparation Time: 10 Minutes

Cooking Time: 22 Minutes

Servings: 9

Ingredients:

- 1 cup cheese
- 1/2 green pepper
- 1/2 cup cottage cheese
- Four slices of bacon
- Pepper
- Salt
- 1 cup red onion
- 1 cup of water
- 1/4 cup whip cream
- 1/4 cup egg whites
- Four eggs

Directions:

1. Blend egg whites, eggs, cream, cheese (cottage), shredded cheese, pepper, and salt within 30 to 45 seconds in a blender.
2. Put the egg mixture into mini muffin cups. Top each with bacon, peppers, and onion.

3. Cover the muffin cups tightly with foil. Place the trivet in the pot and pour 1 cup water.

4. Put the cups on the trivet. Set to steam for 12 minutes. Cooldown before serving.

Nutrition: Calories: 124 Carbs: 3g Protein: 9g Fats: 8

Omelet Bites

Preparation Time: 5 Minutes

Cooking Time: 8 Minutes

Servings: 3

Ingredients:

- One handful mushrooms
- Green onion
- Green peppers
- 1/8 teaspoon hot sauce
- Pepper, salt, mustard, garlic powder
- 1/2 cup cheese cheddar
- 1/2 cup cheese cottage
- Two deli ham slices
- Four eggs

Directions:

1. Whisk eggs, then the cheddar and cottage. Put the ham, veggies, and seasonings; mix.
2. Pour the mixture into greased silicone molds. Put the trivet with the molds in the pot, then fill with 2 cups water.
3. Steam for about 8 minutes. Transfer, cooldown before serving.

Nutrition: Calories: 260 Carbs: 6g Protein: 22g Fats: 16g

Cheddar & Bacon Egg Bites

Preparation Time: 10 Minutes

Cooking Time: 8 Minutes

Servings: 7

Ingredients:

- 1 cup sharp cheddar cheese
- One tablespoon parsley flake
- Four eggs
- Four tablespoons cream
- Hot sauce
- 1 cup of water
- 1/2 cup cheese
- Four slices of bacon

Directions:

1. Blend the cream, cheddar, cottage, and egg in the blender; 30 seconds.
2. Stir in the parsley—grease silicone egg bite molds.
3. Divide the crumbled bacon between them. Put the egg batter into each cup.
4. With a piece of foil, cover each mold. Place the trivet with the molds in the pot, then fill with 1 cup water.
5. Steam for 8 minutes. Remove, let rest for 5 minutes. Serve, sprinkled with black pepper, and optional hot sauce.

Nutrition: Calories: 167 Carbs: 1.5g Protein: 13.5g Fats: 11.7g

Avocado Pico Egg Bites

Preparation Time: 15 Minutes

Cooking Time: 10 Minutes

Servings: 7

Ingredients:

Egg bites:

- 1/ cup cheese cottage
- 1/2 cup cheese Mexican blend
- 1/4 cup cream heavy cream
- 1/4 teaspoon chili powder
- 1/4 teaspoon cumin
- 1/4 teaspoon garlic powder
- Four eggs
- Pepper
- Salt

Pico de Gallo:

- One avocado
- One jalapeno
- 1/2 teaspoon salt
- 1/4 onion
- Two tablespoons cilantro

- Two teaspoons lime juice
- 4 Roma tomatoes

Directions:

1. Mix all of the Pico de Gallo fixing except for the avocado. Gently fold in the avocado.
2. Blend all the egg bites ingredients in a blender. Spoon one tablespoon of Pico de Gallo into each egg bite silicone mold.
3. Place the trivet in the pot, then fill with 1 cup water. Put the molds in the trivet. Set to high within 10 minutes.
4. Remove. Serve topped with cheese and Pico de Gallo.

Nutrition: Calories: 118 Carbs: 1g Protein: 7g Fats: 9g

Buttermilk Griddle Pancakes

Preparation Time: 10 minutes

Cooking Time: 15-20 minutes

Servings: 6

Ingredients:

- 2 cups all-purpose flour
- 3 tbs. granulated sugar
- 2 tsp. baking powder
- 1 tsp. salt
- 1 egg
- 1 1/2 cups buttermilk
- 3 tbs. vegetable oil

Directions:

1. In a mixing bowl, add the all-purpose flour, granulated sugar, baking powder and salt. Stir until combined. Add the egg, buttermilk and vegetable oil. Whisk only until combined. Do not over mix the batter or the pancakes will be tough.

2. Spray a griddle or large skillet with nonstick cooking spray. The temperature of the griddle needs to be about 350°. If using a skillet, place the skillet over medium heat. Do not add the pancake batter until the griddle is hot. Drop the pancakes, by tablespoonfuls, onto the hot griddle.

3. Cook for 1-2 minutes or until bubbles form and pop on the top of the pancakes. Flip the pancakes over and cook for 1 minute or until the pancakes are golden brown. Remove the pancakes from the griddle and serve hot.

Nutrition: Calories: 367 Fat: 15.9g Fiber: 8g Carbs: 39g Protein: 7g

Lemony Parmesan Breadsticks

Preparation Time: 20 minutes

Cooking Time: 25 minutes

Servings: 16

Ingredients

- 1 tablespoon sugar
- 1 (¼-ounce) package active dry yeast
- 1 cup warm water
- 1 cup bran cereal
- 2¼ cups all-purpose flour
- ½ cup Parmesan cheese, shredded
- 1½ teaspoons lemon peel, grated
- 1 teaspoon garlic salt
- 1 teaspoon black pepper
- ½ teaspoon cayenne pepper
- 2 tablespoons olive oil
- Cornmeal, as required
- 1 egg white, slightly beaten

Directions

1. Mix in sugar, yeast and warm water until well blended. Set aside for about 5 minutes.

2. In a food processor, add cereal and pulse until crushed. Add flour, cheese, lemon peel, garlic salt, black pepper and cayenne pepper and pulse for about 10 seconds. Add oil and pulse for about 10 seconds more. Add yeast mixture and pulse a dough ball is formed. Set aside in processor for about 5 minutes. Again, pulse for about 10 seconds more.

3. Remove the dough from the processor and place into a bowl. With a plastic wrap, cover the bowl and set aside for about 10 minutes.

4. Grease and preheat the oven at 325 degrees. Slice the dough into 16 equal sized pieces. Place the dough pieces onto a cornmeal dusted surface and roll each into a thin and 14-inch long rope.

5. Arrange the breadsticks onto prepared baking sheets in a single layer. Brush the top of each breadstick with egg white and set aside for about 15 minutes.

6. Bake for about 25-35 minutes or until top becomes golden brown.

7. Take out from the oven and transfer the baking sheets onto wire racks to cool completely before serving.

Nutrition: 122 Calories 3.5g Total Fat 4.6g Protein 19.1g Carbs

APPETIZER AND SIDES

Coconut Potatoes

Preparation Time: 10 minutes

Cooking Time: 35 minutes

Servings: 8

Ingredients:

- 5 medium sweet potatoes, peeled and sliced into thin rounds
- A pinch of salt and black pepper
- ¼ teaspoon ground nutmeg
- 1 teaspoon fresh thyme, chopped
- 2 garlic cloves, peeled and minced
- 2 cups coconut cream
- 2 tablespoons olive oil

Directions:

1. Heat a small pan with the oil over medium heat, add the cream, and garlic, stir, bring to a simmer, and cook for 5 minutes. In a roasting pan, combine the potatoes with the thyme with salt, pepper and the nutmeg, stir, drizzle the coconut cream mixture all over potatoes and bake covered at 400ºF for 15 minutes. Uncover the baking dish, cook for 15 minutes more, divide between plates, and serve.

Nutrition: 340 Calories 4g Fat 3g Fiber 20g Carbs 7g Protein

Sweet Potato and Walnuts Mix

Preparation Time: 10 minutes

Cooking Time: 50 minutes

Servings: 4

Ingredients:

- 4 sweet potatoes, cubed
- 1½ cups cranberries
- 1 tablespoon extra-virgin olive oil
- ½ cup coconut cream
- A pinch of salt and black pepper
- ¼ cup walnuts, crushed

Directions:

1. Arrange the potato cubes on a baking sheet, add oil, salt and pepper, toss and bake at 350ºF for 40 minutes. Heat a pan over medium heat, add the cranberries, and cook for 3-4 minutes stirring often. Add roasted potato cubes and the rest of the ingredients, toss, cook for 5 more minutes, divide between plates and serve.

Nutrition: 223 Calories 8g Fat 5.5g Fiber 20g Carbs 5g Protein

Roasted Squash

Preparation Time: 10 minutes

Cooking Time: 40 minutes

Servings: 4

Ingredients:

- 2 tablespoons olive oil
- Salt and ground black pepper, to taste
- 8 cups butternut squash, cubed
- 1 tablespoon sweet paprika

Directions:

1. In a roasting pan, mix the squash with the oil and the rest of the ingredients, toss, bake at 400°F for 40 minutes, divide between plates and serve.

Nutrition: 90 Calories 3g Fat 4g Fiber 14g Carbs 3g Protein

Squash Puree

Preparation Time: 10 minutes

Cooking Time: 1 hour

Servings: 4

Ingredients:

- 1 butternut squash, halved
- Salt and ground black pepper, to taste
- 4 eggs, whites and yolks separated
- ½ cup coconut milk

Directions:

1. Arrange the squash halves on a lined baking sheet, salt and black pepper, bake in the oven at 350ºF for 20 minutes, take the squash out of the oven and scoop the flesh into a blender. Add the rest of the ingredients, blend well and transfer the mixture to a baking dish. Bake in the oven at 350ºF, bake for 40 minutes, divide between plates and serve.

Nutrition: 203 Calories 13g Fat 2g Fiber 16g Carbs 4g Protein

Walnut Cauliflower Rice Mix

Preparation Time: 10 minutes

Cooking Time: 20 minutes

Servings: 8

Ingredients:

- 2 cauliflower heads, florets separated
- 1 tablespoon olive oil
- 1 onion, peeled and chopped
- 4 celery stalks, chopped
- 1 garlic clove, peeled and minced
- 3 cups mushrooms, chopped
- 2½ teaspoons dried sage
- ½ cup walnuts, chopped
- Salt and ground black pepper, to taste

Directions:

1. Put the cauliflower in a food processor and pulse a bit. Heat a pan with the oil over medium-high heat, add the garlic, onions, and celery, stir and cook for 5 minutes. Add the cauliflower and the rest of the ingredients, toss, cook for 15 more minutes, divide between plates and serve.

Nutrition: 120 Calories 3g Fat 4g Fiber 4g Carbs 7g Protein

LUNCH

Figs and Goat Cheese-Stuffed Chicken

Preparation Time: 20 Minutes

Cooking Time: 8 Hours

Servings: 4

Ingredients:

- 4 x 4oz chicken breasts
- 4 figs
- ½ cup goat cheese, crumbled
- 1 tsp salt
- 1 tsp black pepper
- Extra virgin olive oil

Directions:

1. Combine 3 tbsp olive oil, salt, black pepper in a bowl, and rub onto chicken breasts. Marinate for an hour.
2. Remove fig skin, and slice figs into ½" pieces. Combine with goat cheese.
3. Turn slow cooker to Low.

4. Place plastic wrap over chicken breasts and pound with a mallet until each breast is approximately ¼″ thick (or ask your butcher to do it).

5. Scoop a quarter of the cheese-fig mixture into the chicken, roll up chicken breast, and place in a slow cooker.

6. Repeat for each chicken breast.

7. Cook on low for 8 hours.

8. Serve with a green salad.

Nutrition: Calories 369 Carbs 7 g Fat 18 g Protein 46 g Sodium 811 mg

Carne Asada

Preparation Time: 10 Minutes

Cooking Time: 8 Hours

Servings: 8

Ingredients:

- 4 lb. chuck roast
- 1 onion, chopped
- Four limes, juiced
- ½ cup cilantro, minced
- Eight cloves garlic, minced
- 2 tsp paprika
- 2 tsp oregano
- 2 tsp cumin
- 2 tsp salt
- 1 tsp black pepper

Directions:

1. Rinse pot roast and pat dry.
2. Combine remaining fixings in a blender, and mix until well combined.
3. Brush slow cooker with extra virgin olive oil, and set on high.
4. Coat pot roast with cilantro topping.
5. Place in a slow cooker, and cook for 8 hours.
6. Serve with Cauliflower Rice.

Nutrition: Calories 506 Carbs 3 g Fat 19 g Protein 75 g Sodium 733 mg

Amazing Pulled Pork

Preparation Time: 25 Minutes

Cooking Time: 8 Hours

Servings: 8

Ingredients:

- 5 lb. pork shoulder
- 2 tbsp mustard
- 2 cups tomato purée
- 6 Medjool Dates, pitted
- ½ tsp cloves, ground
- ½ tsp cinnamon
- 2 tsp salt
- Extra virgin olive oil
- Tortilla Wraps
- Eight eggs
- 1 tbsp coconut flour
- ½ tsp salt

Directions:

1. Place pitted dates in a blender, mix until paste forms, add tomato purée, cinnamon, salt, black pepper, and mix. Combine mustard, blended tomato puree, cloves, cinnamon, salt, and mix.

2. Place pork shoulder in a slow cooker, pour the sauce into a slow cooker, and coat pork shoulder—Cook pork for 8 hours on high.
3. Once the pork is cooked, use a fork to shred.
4. For tortilla wraps, whisk eggs, add milk and flour, and mix until well combined.
5. Heat 4 tbsp oil in a skillet on medium-high.
6. Pour 1/8th of the mixture into skillet and cook each side 30 seconds.
7. Spoon pork mixture into egg tortilla and serve.

Nutrition: Calories 777 Carbs 8 g Fat 55 g Protein 59 g Sodium 835 mg

Braised Pork Belly

Preparation Time: 10 Minutes

Cooking Time: 4 Hours

Servings: 8

Ingredients:

- 1 lb. pork belly
- Two medium onions, diced
- 1 tsp Dijon mustard
- ½ cup apple sauce
- 1 tsp black pepper
- 1 tsp salt

Directions:

1. Heat extra virgin olive oil in the skillet, add onion, sauté for a minute.
2. Place onion in a slow cooker, add pork belly, apple sauce—cook on high for 4 hours.
3. Serve with Walnut Cabbage Salad.

Nutrition: Calories 278 Carbs 3.5 g Fat 15 g Protein 26 g Sodium 1214 mg

DINNER

Low-Carb Pork Medallions

Preparation Time: 15 Minutes

Cooking Time: 20 Minutes

Servings: 2

Ingredients:

- 1 lb. pork tenderloin
- Three medium shallots
- ¼ cup oil

Directions:

1. Cut the meat into half-inch-thick slices.
2. Cleave the shallots and put them on a plate.
3. Warm the oil in a skillet.
4. Press each piece of pork into the shallots on both sides. The shallots will stick to the pork if you press firmly.
5. Put the meat slices, coated with shallots, into the warm oil and cook till carried out.
6. Some of the shallots will burn during cooking, but they'll give a heavenly taste to the red meat.

7. Simply cook the beef until it's cooked through.

8. Serve with vegetables.

Nutrition: Calories 519 Fat 4 g Carbs 7 g Protein 46 g

Rosemary Roast Beef and White Radishes

Preparation Time: 10 Minutes

Cooking Time: 60 Minutes

Servings: 8

Ingredients:

- 3 lb. boneless beef roast
- Two white daikon radishes
- 3 tbsp. rosemary
- 2 tbsp. salt to taste
- 2 tbsp. olive oil

Directions:

1. Preheat oven to 400 F.
2. Spread olive oil, rosemary, and salt over the beef.
3. Put the stripped and severed radishes at the base of a warming dish.
4. Put the beef on the radishes and bake for one hour.
5. When done, wrap the burger in foil and let rest for 20 minutes before serving.

Nutrition: Calories 492 Fat 39 g Carbs 4.1 g Protein 29 g

Bacon-Wrapped Pork Chops

Preparation Time: 10 Minutes

Cooking Time: 30 Minutes

Servings: 4

Ingredients:

- 12 oz. bacon package
- 6 to 8 boneless pork chops
- Salt and pepper

Directions:

1. Preheat your oven to 350 F
2. On a plate or cutting board, layout the pork chops.
3. Wrap each piece of pork in uncooked bacon cuts.
4. Place each bacon-wrapped pork chop onto the baking sheet.
5. Crush extra pepper over the highest point of the now bacon-wrapped pork.
6. Heat them for 30 minutes, flipping them at the 15-minute imprint. Serve promptly and appreciate it!

Nutrition: Calories 350 Fat 2.8 g Carbs 2.4 g Protein 8 g

Rosemary Chicken with Avocado Sauce

Preparation Time: 4 Minutes

Cooking Time: 18 Minutes

Servings: 4

Ingredients:

- 1 avocado, pitted
- ½ cup mayonnaise
- 3 tbsp. ghee
- Four chicken breasts
- Salt and black pepper to taste
- 1 cup rosemary, chopped
- ½ cup chicken broth

Directions:

1. Spoon avocado, mayonnaise, and salt into a food processor and puree until it is a smooth sauce. Season to taste with salt. Pour sauce into a jar and refrigerate.
2. Melt ghee in a large skillet, season chicken with salt and black pepper, and fry for 4 minutes on each side to a golden brown. Remove chicken to a plate.
3. Pour broth into the same skillet and add cilantro. Bring to simmer for 3 minutes and add chicken.
4. Cover and cook on low heat for 5 minutes until the liquid has reduced. Dish chicken only into serving plates and spoon the

mayo-avocado sauce over. Serve warm with buttered green beans and baby carrots.

Nutrition: Calories 398 Fat 32 g Carbs 4 g Protein 24g

Crispy Chicken Nuggets

Preparation Time: 5 Minutes

Cooking Time: 20 Minutes

Servings: 4

Ingredients:

- 2 tbsp. ranch dressing
- ½ cup almond flour
- 1 egg
- 2 tbsp. garlic powder
- Four chicken breasts, cubed
- Salt and black pepper to taste
- 1 tbsp. butter, melted

Directions:

1. Preheat oven to 400 F, then grease a baking dish with the butter.
2. In a bowl, combine salt, garlic powder, flour, and pepper, and stir. In a separate bowl, beat egg.
3. Add the chicken to the egg mixture, then coat with the flour mixture. Bake for 18-20 minutes, turning halfway through. Remove to paper towels, drain the excess grease, and serve with ranch dressing.

Nutrition: Calories 473 Fat 31 g Carbs 7.6 g Protein 43 g

Zucchini & Bell Pepper Chicken Gratin

Preparation Time: 5 Minutes

Cooking Time: 40 Minutes

Servings: 5

Ingredients:

- One red bell pepper, sliced
- 1 zucchini, chopped
- Salt and black pepper to taste
- 1 tsp. garlic powder
- 1 tbsp. olive oil
- Five chicken breasts, skinless and boneless, sliced
- 1 tomato, chopped
- ½ tsp. dried oregano
- ½ tsp. dried basil
- ½ cup mozzarella cheese, shredded

Directions:

1. Coat the chicken with salt, black pepper, and garlic powder. Warm olive oil in a skillet over medium heat and add the chicken slices. Cook until golden and remove to a baking dish.
2. To the same pan, add the zucchini, tomato, bell pepper, basil, oregano, and salt, cook for 2 minutes, and spread

over the chicken. Bake in the oven at 360 F for 20 minutes.

3. Sprinkle the mozzarella over the chicken, return to the oven, and bake for 5 minutes more until the cheese is melted and bubbling.

Nutrition: Calories 467 Fat 23.5 g Carbs 6.2 g Protein 45.7 g

Coconut Chicken with Creamy Asparagus Sauce

Preparation Time: 5 Minutes

Cooking Time: 25 Minutes

Servings: 4

Ingredients:

- 2 tbsp. butter
- 1-pound chicken thighs
- 2 tbsp. coconut oil
- 2 tbsp. coconut flour
- 2 cups asparagus, chopped
- 1 tsp. oregano
- 1 cup heavy cream
- 1 cup chicken broth

Directions:

1. Heat a frypan over medium heat
2. Add the coconut oil to melt. Brown the chicken on all sides, approximately 6-8 minutes. Set aside.
3. Melt the butter and whisk in the flour over medium heat. Whisk in the heavy cream and chicken broth and bring to a boil. Stir in oregano.

4. Add the asparagus to the skillet, then cook for 10 minutes until tender. Handover to a food processor and pulse until smooth. Season with salt and pepper. Return to the skillet and add the chicken; cook for 5 minutes and serve.

Nutrition: Calories 451 Fat 36.7 g Carbs 3.2 g Protein 18.5 g

Herb Pork Chops with Cranberry Sauce

Preparation Time: 5 Minutes

Cooking Time: 2 Hours and 40 Minutes

Servings: 2

Ingredients:

- Four pork chops
- ½ tsp. garlic powder
- Salt and black pepper to taste
- 1 tsp. fresh basil, chopped
- A drizzle of olive oil
- ½ onion, chopped
- ½ cup white wine
- Juice of ½ lemon
- 1 bay leaf
- 1 cup chicken stock
- Fresh parsley, chopped, for serving
- 1 cup cranberries
- ½ tsp. fresh rosemary, chopped
- ½ cup xylitol
- ½ cup of water
- ½ tsp. harissa paste sriracha sauce

Directions:

1. Preheat oven to 360 F.

2. In a bowl, combine the pork chops with basil, salt, garlic powder, and black pepper. Heat a pan with a drizzle of oil over medium heat, put the pork in, and cook until browned, about 4-5 minutes; set aside.

3. Stir in the onion and cook for 2 minutes.

4. Next, you need to add the bay leaf and wine and cook for 4 minutes.

5. Pour in lemon juice and chicken stock and simmer for 5 minutes.

6. Return the pork and cook for 10 minutes. Cover the pan and put it in the oven for 2 hours.

7. Set a pan over medium-high heat, add the cranberries, rosemary, sriracha sauce, water, and xylitol, and bring to a simmer for 15 minutes.

8. Take away the pork chops from the oven and discard the bay leaf. Pour the sauce over the pork and serve sprinkled with parsley.

Nutrition: Calories 450 Fat 23.5 g Carbs 7.3 g Protein 42 g

Pork Chops with Basil Tomato Sauce

Preparation Time: 10 Minutes

Cooking Time: 40 Minutes

Servings: 4

Ingredients:

- Four pork chops
- ½ tbsp. fresh basil, chopped
- 1 garlic clove, minced
- 1 tbsp. olive oil
- 7 oz. canned diced tomatoes
- ½ tbsp. tomato paste
- Salt and black pepper to taste
- ½ red chili, finely chopped

Directions:

1. Season the pork with black pepper and salt. Set a pan over medium heat and warm oil, put in the pork chops, cook for 3 minutes, turn and cook for another 3 minutes; remove to a bowl. Add the garlic and cook for 30 seconds.

2. Stir in the tomato paste, tomatoes, and chili; bring to a boil, and reduce heat to medium-low. Put in the pork chops, cover the pan, and simmer everything for 30

minutes. Remove the pork chops to plates and sprinkle with fresh oregano to serve.

Nutrition: Calories 425 Fat 25 g Carbs 2.5 g Protein 39 g

Citrus Pork with Sautéed Cabbage & Tomatoes

Preparation Time: 7 Minutes

Cooking Time: 20 Minutes

Servings: 4

Ingredients:

- 3 tbsp. olive oil
- 2 tbsp. lemon juice
- 1 garlic clove, pureed
- Four pork loin chops
- 1/3 head cabbage, shredded
- 1 tomato, chopped
- 1 tbsp. white wine
- Salt and black pepper to taste
- ¼ tsp. cumin
- ¼ tsp. ground nutmeg
- 1 tbsp. parsley

Directions:

1. In a bowl, blend the lemon juice, garlic, salt, pepper, and olive oil. Brush the pork with the mixture.

2. Preheat grill to high heat. Grill the pork for 2-3 minutes on each side until cooked through. Remove to serving plates. Warm the remaining olive oil in a pan and cook cabbage for 5 minutes.

3. Drizzle with white wine, sprinkle with cumin, nutmeg, salt, and pepper. Add the tomatoes, then cook for another 5 minutes, stirring occasionally.

4. Spoon the sautéed cabbage to the side of the chops and serve sprinkled with parsley.

Nutrition: Calories 565 Fat 36.7 g Carbs 6.1 g Protein 43 g

SOUP AND STEWS

Cream of Broccoli Soup

Preparation Time: 10 minutes

Cooking Time: 35 minutes

Servings: 4

Ingredients:

- 1 tablespoon olive oil
- 1 medium white onion, chopped
- 2 cloves minced garlic
- 3 cups chicken broth (low sodium)
- 1-pound fresh chopped broccoli
- 1 medium leek, sliced (white and light green parts only)
- Salt and pepper
- 1 cup canned coconut milk

Directions:

1. Heat the oil in a large saucepan over medium-high heat. Add the onions and cook for 4 to 5 minutes until translucent. Stir in the garlic and cook for 1 minute more.

2. Add the broth, broccoli, and leeks then season with salt and pepper. Bring to a boil then reduce heat and simmer for 20 minutes until the broccoli is very tender. Turn off the heat and puree the soup using an immersion blender. Stir in the coconut milk and adjust seasoning to taste. Serve hot.

Nutrition: 210 Calories 19g Carbs 13g Fat 4g Protein

Chicken Tortilla Soup

Preparation Time: 20 minutes

Cooking Time: 25 minutes

Servings: 8

Ingredients:

- 2 cans black beans
- 1 can corn
- 1-2 C shredded chicken breast
- 2 cans tomatoes and green chilies
- Garlic
- Black pepper
- Cumin
- Chili powder
- Chicken stock
- Tortilla chips
- Avocado garnish
- Sour cream garnish
- Cheese garnish

Directions:

1. To the pot of broth add black beans, corn, and cup of reserved chicken. Cover and simmer on lowest setting

for one hour, stirring occasionally. Serve with tortilla chips and avocado, cheese, and sour cream garnish.

Nutrition: 260 calories 4g fats 5.9g fiber

Italian Sausage and Potato Soup

Preparation Time: 25 minutes

Cooking Time: 35 minutes

Servings: 8

Ingredients:

- Lb. Ground Italian sausage
- 8 Medium Yukon Gold potatoes
- 6 C chopped fresh Tuscan kale
- 1 Large yellow onion
- 4 Garlic cloves
- 1 TBSP. Black pepper
- 1 TBSP. Salt
- 4 TBSP. Dried oregano
- 1 TBSP. Garlic powder
- 1 TBSP. Onion powder
- 1 tsp. Nutmeg
- C half and half
- 8 C low sodium chicken broth
- C water
- TBSP. Olive oil

Directions:

1   Wash all veggies and dry. Slice potatoes into ¼ inch round slices, don't peel. Loosely chop Kale. Mince garlic. Dice Onion. In a large pot heat olive oil and brown sausage. Add potatoes and salt and pepper. Cook five minutes then add garlic, onion, and all your seasonings. Sweat garlic and onion 5 minutes then add broth, water, and half and half. Stirring constantly, bring to a slow boil. Reduce heat to low and cover. Simmer 20 minutes then add kale. Simmer 30 minutes stirring frequently.

Nutrition: 260 calories 6g fats 3g fiber

Beef and Barley Soup

Preparation Time: 25 minutes

Cooking Time: 35 minutes

Servings: 8

Ingredients:

- 8 C Beef Stock
- C Water
- 1.5 Lb. Large grind sirloin
- 1 Medium yellow onion
- Large carrots
- 1 C Whole organic barley
- Whole garlic cloves
- 2 tsp Black pepper
- 2 tsp Salt
- 2 tsp Adolf's meat tenderizer
- 1 tsp Garlic powder
- 1 TBSP Onion powder
- 2 TBSP Dried onion flakes
- ¼ C Olive oil

Directions:

1 Tenderize beef with either a good pounding or some meat tenderizer.

2   Wash and slice and dice all veggies. In a large pot heat olive oil and add veggies, sweating for approximately 7-9 minutes on medium-low heat. Add beef and brown but don't cook all the way through. Add broth and cover.

3   Simmer on low-medium for approximately 20 minutes. Add water and barley and increase heat to high. Cook uncovered for 15 minutes then reduce heat to low and cover. Simmer for 20 minutes stirring occasionally.

4   For the last five minutes simmer uncovered. Serve with a nice hot crusty French bread.

Nutrition: 250 calories 6g fats 3g fiber

Taco Soup

Preparation Time: 25 minutes

Cooking Time: 35 minutes

Servings: 8

Ingredients:

- 1 Lb. Ground beef
- 1 block Mexican Velveeta
- 1 Can Evaporated milk
- 1 Box Noodle Soup (both packets)
- 10 C Chicken stock or water
- Can Green chilies and tomatoes
- 1 TBSP Cumin
- 1 TBSP Black pepper
- 1 tsp Salt
- 1 TBSP Garlic powder
- Tortilla Chips (for garnish)

Directions:

1   In a large pot, brown ground beef with all seasoning and a little broth or water to blend well. Add both cans of green chilies and tomatoes. Simmer for 5 minutes. Cut Velveeta into cubes.

2   Add broth and milk to pot then stir in cheese cubes. Stir frequently. Serve with tortilla chips. We love this soup with peperoni bread! (recipe above)

Nutrition: 249 calories 3g fats 6g fiber

Chicken and Sausage Gumbo

Preparation Time: 30 minutes

Cooking Time: 45 minutes

Servings: 8

Ingredients:

- Boneless skinless chicken breasts
- 1 Lb. Andouille sausage
- 10 C Chicken or Veggie broth
- Large carrots
- Celery stalks
- 1 Medium Yellow onion
- Fresh Bay leaves
- ¼ C Olive or vegetable oil
- 2 TBSP Old Bay seasoning
- 1 TBSP Cajun seasoning
- 2 TBSP Louisiana or Tabasco hot sauce
- 1 tsp Salt

- 1 TBSP Garlic powder
- 1 TBSP Onion powder
- 1 TBSP Onion flakes
- 1 TBSP Poultry season
- 1 TBSP Dried parsley
- TBSP+ Flour
- 1 C Whole grain white rice

Directions:

1. Wash and dice all veggies and set aside. Cut chicken and sausage into bite-sized pieces. In a large pot heat oil to medium and add meats. Brown slightly on both sides then add all veggies and seasoning and herbs. Sprinkle flour in bottom of pot and with a wooden spoon or spatula, while scraping bottom of pot, make a thick pasty roux. Brown the roux to the color you want your gumbo. Then, gradually add 2 cups broth and stir to blend well until you have a thick gravy. Simmer for 10 minutes.

2. Turn up the heat and add the rest of the broth and the rice. Simmer on low for 30 minutes. Serve with a side of white rice or cornbread!

VEGETABLES

Asian Vegetable Array with Quinoa Salad

Preparation Time: 15 minutes

Cooking Time: 5 minutes

Servings: 2

Ingredients:

- 1 cup chopped red cabbage
- 1/2 cup shredded carrots
- 1 red bell pepper, chopped
- 1 cup diced cucumber
- Shell cup shelled and cooked edamame
- 1/4 teaspoon salt
- cups water
- 1 cup quinoa
- For the dressing:
- 1 tablespoon sesame oil
- 1/4 cup soy sauce
- tablespoon rice wine vinegar
- 1/4 cup chopped cilantro

- tablespoons chopped green onion
- 1/4 teaspoon grated ginger
- 1 tablespoon sesame seeds
- Salt and black pepper, to taste
- 1/8 teaspoon red pepper flakes

Directions:

1 Pour the water into a medium sauce pan and add the salt and quinoa and bring it to a boil. Once the quinoa has boiled for around 6 minutes turn the heat down to low and simmer until the water has been absorbed (this could take around 14 to 16 minutes.) Remove the cooked quinoa from the heat, use a fork and poke it around to fluff it. Use a large bowl to place the quinoa in then add in the cucumber, carrots, red pepper, edamame, and cabbage. Gently mix and set aside. Make the dressing by whisking together the sesame oil, soy sauce, rice wine vinegar, cilantro, green onions, ginger, sesame seeds, red pepper flakes, pepper and salt. Gently mix the dressing into the quinoa salad combine everything well. Serve at room temperature or chilled.

Nutrition: 105 calories 3g fiber 12g fats

Barely and Squash Salad

Preparation Time: 10 minutes

Cooking Time: 15 minutes

Serving: 2

Ingredients:

- oz pearl barley
- 1 tbsp olive oil
- 3.5 oz sun dried tomatoes
- 1 small red onion
- 10.5 oz broccoli cut into medium-size pieces
- 1 tbsp small capers
- 14 black olives, pitted
- tbsp pumpkin seeds
- 1 oz pack basil
- 1 butternut squash
- For the dressing:
- tbsp extra-virgin olive oil
- tbsp balsamic vinegar
- 1 garlic clove crushed or grated
- 1 tbsp Dijon mustard

Directions:

1 Pre-heat the oven to 400 degrees. Take a baking tray and place the squash on it spread olive oil over the squash and toss. Roast the squash for about 20 minutes. In the meantime, cook the barley by boiling it in salted water until its tender but still firm (for about 28 minutes). Make the dressing by whisking all the ingredients in a small bowl and then seasoning it with salt and pepper as desired. When the barley is ready drain and then put it in a nice salad bowl or tray. Pour the dressing over the barely and mix it well and set it aside to chill. Blanch the broccoli in salted boiling water until it is tender, rinse it in cold water, drain well and then add it to the barley; mix well. Add the roasted squash, sun dried tomatoes, the basil, the sliced onion, capers, black olives pumpkin seeds and basil; combine everything well. Serve warm or cold.

Nutrition: 114 calories 14g fats 3g fiber

Grilled Veggies and Pasta Salad

Preparation Time: 15 minutes

Cooking Time: 10 minutes

Serving: 2

Ingredients:

- small bulbs fennel
- 1/4 cup chopped fennel fronds
- 1 small head radicchio
- baby bell peppers seeded and cut in halves
- Kosher salt and freshly ground pepper
- 1/2 cup extra-virgin olive oil
- 8 ounces orecchiette
- tablespoons chopped fresh parsley
- 1 15 -ounce can cannellini beans
- ounces parmesan cheese
- Juice of 1 lemon

Directions:

1 Get the grill or grill pan ready, preheat it to medium high. Toss the fennel wedges, the radicchio and the bell peppers with ¼ cup of olive oil in a large bowl then season it with pepper and salt. Place the vegetables on the grill and grill them turning them over sometimes

until they are crisp, tender and charred. The peppers and radicchio should take about 4 minutes and the fennel about 6 minutes. Remove the vegetables from the grill and allow them to cool, and then cut them into small pieces. Cook the pasta in a large pot of salted boiling water (cook for about 2 minutes less than the label directs, it must be al dente) Drain and rinse the pasta under cool water, drain again and then put the pasta in a serving bowl. Add in the cannellini beans, the grilled vegetables, the lemon juice, the remaining ¼ cup of olive oil, the parsley, pepper to taste and the salt; toss. Add in the fennel fronds and the parmesan shavings gently fold into the salad and then serve.

Nutrition: 120 calories 13g fats 2g fiber

Rustic Potato and Egg Salad

Preparation Time: 10 minutes

Cooking Time: 10 minutes

Serving: 2

Ingredients:

- bacon rashers
- eggs
- 12 small coliban potatoes 3
- 0g drained gherkins
- green shallots
- 1/4 cup loosely packed
- fresh dill
- small garlic clove
- 40g sour cream
- 60g good-quality mayonnaise
- Salt & freshly ground black pepper
- tablespoons finely chopped capers

Directions:

1　Boil the potatoes uncovered until tender in salted water in a large saucepan. This should take about 10 minutes. (To check if the potatoes are ready pierce them with a skewer.) When the potatoes are ready drain them and set them aside to cool for about 20 to 30 minutes. Cut the potatoes into halves and place them in a large serving / salad bowl. Boil the eggs uncovered for about 12 minutes (medium-hard boiled) drain them and run cold water over them. Peel them and set them aside. Place a non-stick frying pan over high heat and when the pan is hot, stir in the bacon and cook it until crisp. Remove from heat and place the bacon over paper towels. Put the sour cream, mayonnaise and garlic in small bowl and whisk together. Add the capers, green shallots, dill and gherkin to the salad bowl with the potatoes; toss a little and then add in the sour cream sauce and toss again combining everything well. Add in the bacon and a little season of salt and pepper and toss once more. Quarter-cut the eggs and then arrange them nicely on top of the potato salad season with salt and pepper and serve.

Nutrition: 118 calories 2g protein 10g fats

Roasted and Fresh Vegetable Salad

Preparation Time: 10 minutes

Cooking Time: 20 minutes

Servings: 2

Ingredients:

- medium beets
- medium carrots
- 1zucchini
- 1 glove of crushed garlic
- 1 medium onion sliced
- Olive oil
- 1 teaspoon of freshly squeezed lemon
- 1 tablespoon of butter
- 1 teaspoon of red wine vinegar
- Thyme
- Salt and Pepper
- ½ cup of goat cheese
- 1 small lettuce

Directions:

1 Use a very sharp knife to cut the tops off of the beets. Then peel them (or scrub off peel), then cut them in to thin small sticks, like French fries (may want to use clear

or latex gloves to not stain hands). Cut the tops off of the carrots and peel them; then also cut into thin small sticks. Cut the tops off of the zucchini and cut lengthwise in 3 equal pieces and then quarter cut each piece. Cover a baking tray with a large piece of tin foil and spread the beets, carrots and zucchini over it. Drizzle olive oil and the crushed garlic on the top (may need to spread / move the veggies around so they all get a little tinge of garlic.) Sprinkle the teaspoon lemon juice over the vegetables and season with salt, pepper, and thyme. Preheat the oven to 450 degrees and roast the vegetables (around 30 minutes or until tender). Then remove from oven and chill. Place a small frying pan over medium heat and melt the 1 tablespoon of butter add the onion slices and sauté them until golden then season with a little salt and pepper and the teaspoon of vinegar. Remove from heat. Wash and dry the lettuce and then shred it into a nice salad bowl season the lettuce with a drizzle of olive oil and a drizzle of red wine vinegar. Top the lettuce with the roasted vegetables and toss then add in the sautéed onions and goat cheese; serve.

Nutrition: 115 calories 13g fats 1g protein

Strawberry, Almonds and Lettuce Salad

Preparation Time: 10 minutes

Cooking Time: 10 minutes

Servings: 2

Ingredients:

- 1 Bermuda onion
- pint fresh strawberries
- Feta cheese as desired
- bunches fresh spinach
- romaine lettuce
- ½ cup of chopped almonds
- For the sauce:
- tablespoons poppy seeds
- 1/3 cup mayonnaise
- 1/3 cup sour cream
- 1/4 cup white sugar
- tablespoons white wine vinegar
- Salt and pepper as desired

Directions:

1   Combine the spinach, romaine lettuce, sliced onions, almonds and strawberries in a large bowl Take a small bowl and combine the sour cream, mayonnaise, poppy

seeds, sugar and vinegar and whisk well, you could also pour it in a jar with a tight lid and shake it back and forth. Taste and if necessary, add salt or pepper. Pour sauce over the salad and toss until well combined.

Nutrition: 119 calories 15g carbs 3g fiber

SNACK AND DESSERTS

Curry Spiced Almonds

Preparation Time: 5 Minutes

Cooking Time: 25 Minutes

Servings: 4

Ingredients:

- 1 cup whole almonds
- Two teaspoons olive oil
- 1 teaspoon curry powder
- ¼ teaspoon salt
- ¼ teaspoon ground turmeric
- Pinch cayenne

Directions:

1. Preheat the oven to 300 F
2. In a mixing bowl, whisk the spices and olive oil.
3. Toss in the almonds, then spread on the baking sheet.
4. Bake for 25 minutes until toasted, then cool and store in an airtight container.

Nutrition: Calories 155 Fat 14g Protein 5g Net Carbs 2g

Chia Peanut Butter Bites

Preparation Time: 10 Minutes

Cooking Time: 10 Minutes

Servings: 6

Ingredients:

- ½ ounce of raw almonds
- One tablespoon powdered erythritol
- Four teaspoons coconut oil
- Two tablespoons canned coconut milk
- ½ teaspoon vanilla extract
- Two tablespoons chia seeds, ground to powder
- ¼ cup coconut cream

Directions:

1. Put the almonds in a skillet over medium-low heat, and cook until toasted. Takes about 5 minutes.
2. Transfer the almonds to a food processor with the erythritol and one teaspoon coconut oil.
3. Blend until it forms a smooth almond butter.
4. Heat the rest of the coconut oil in a skillet over medium heat.
5. Add the coconut milk and vanilla and bring to a simmer.

6. Stir in the ground chia seeds, coconut cream, and almond butter.

7. Cook for 2 minutes, then spread in a foil-lined square dish.

8. Chill until the mixture is firm, then cut into squares to serve.

Nutrition: Calories 110 Fat 8g Protein 2g Net Carbs 7g

Cheesy Sausage Dip

Preparation Time: 10 Minutes

Cooking Time: 2 Hours

Servings: 12

Ingredients:

- ½ pound ground Italian sausage
- ½ cup diced tomatoes
- Two green onions, sliced thin
- 4 ounces cream cheese, cubed
- 4 ounces pepper jack cheese, cubed
- 1 cup sour cream

Directions:

1. Brown the sausage in a skillet, wait for it to cook completely, then stir in the tomatoes.
2. Cook for 2 minutes, stirring often, then stir in the green onions.
3. Line the bottom of a slow cooker with the cheeses, then spoon the sausage mixture on top.
4. Spoon the sour cream over the sausage, then cover and cook on high heat for 2 hours, stirring once halfway through.
5. Serve with celery sticks or pork rinds for dipping.

Nutrition: Calories 170 Fat 15g Protein 7g Net Carbs 2g

Salted Kale Chips

Preparation Time: 10 Minutes

Cooking Time: 12 Minutes

Servings: 2

Ingredients:

- ½ bunch fresh kale
- 1 tablespoon olive oil
- Salt and pepper to taste

Directions:

1. Preheat the oven to 350 F and line a baking sheet with foil.
2. Fit the thick stems from the kale and then tear the leaves into pieces.
3. Toss the kale with olive oil and spread it on the baking sheet.
4. Bake for 10 to 12 minutes until crisp, then sprinkle with salt and pepper.

Nutrition: Calories 75 Fat 7g Protein 1g Net Carbs 3g

Bacon Jalapeno Quick Bread

Preparation Time: 20 Minutes

Cooking Time: 45 Minutes

Servings: 10

Ingredients:

- Four slices of thick-cut bacon
- Three jalapeno peppers
- ½ cup coconut flour sifted
- ½ teaspoon baking soda
- ½ teaspoon salt
- Six large eggs, beaten
- ½ cup coconut oil, melted
- ¼ cup of water

Directions:

1. Preheat the oven to 400 F
2. Grease a loaf pan with cooking spray.
3. Spread the bacon and jalapenos on a baking sheet and roast for 10 minutes, stirring halfway through.
4. Crumble the bacon and cut the jalapenos in half to remove the seeds.
5. Combine the bacon and jalapeno in a food processor and pulse until well chopped.

6. Beat together the coconut flour, baking soda, and salt in a bowl.
7. Add the eggs, coconut oil, and water, then stir in the bacon and jalapenos.
8. Spread in the loaf pan, then bake for 40 to 45 minutes until a knife inserted in the center comes out clean.

Nutrition: Calories 225 Fat 19g Protein 8g Net Carbs 3g

Toasted Pumpkin Seeds

Preparation Time: 5 Minutes

Cooking Time: 5 Minutes

Servings: 2

Ingredients:

- ½ cup hulled pumpkin seeds
- Two teaspoons coconut oil
- Two teaspoons chili powder
- ½ teaspoon salt

Directions:

1. Heat a cast-iron skillet over medium heat.
2. Add the pumpkin seeds and let them cook until toasted, about 3 to 5 minutes, stirring often.
3. Remove from heat and stir in the coconut oil, chili powder, and salt.
4. Let the seeds cool, then store in an airtight container.

Nutrition: Calories 100 Fat 8.5g Protein 5.5g Net Carbs 0.5g

Bacon-Wrapped Burger Bites

Preparation Time: 5 Minutes

Cooking Time: 60 Minutes

Servings: 6

Ingredients:

- 6 ounces ground beef (80% lean)
- ¼ teaspoon onion powder
- ¼ teaspoon garlic powder
- ¼ teaspoon ground cumin
- Salt and pepper to taste
- Six slices bacon, uncooked

Directions:

1. Preheat the oven to 350 F
2. Combine the onion powder, garlic powder, cumin, salt, and pepper in a bowl.
3. Add the beef and stir until well combined.
4. Divide the ground beef mixture into six even portions and roll them into balls.
5. Wrap each ball with a slice of bacon and place it on the baking sheet.
6. Bake for 60 minutes until the bacon is crisp and the beef is cooked through.

Nutrition: Calories 150 Fat 10g Protein 16g Net Carbs 0.5g

Almond Sesame Crackers

Preparation Time: 10 Minutes

Cooking Time: 15 Minutes

Servings: 6

Ingredients:

- 1 ½ cups almond flour
- ½ cup sesame seeds
- 1 teaspoon dried oregano
- ½ teaspoon salt
- 1 large egg, whisked
- One tablespoon coconut oil, melted

Directions:

1. Preheat the oven to 350 F
2. Whisk together the almond flour, sesame seeds, oregano, and salt in a bowl.
3. Add the eggs and coconut oil, stirring into a soft dough.
4. Sandwich the dough between two sheets of parchment and roll to 1/8 thickness.
5. Cut into squares and arrange them on the baking sheet.
6. Bake for 10 to 12 minutes or wait until browned around the edges.

Nutrition: Calories 145 Fat 12.5g Protein 5g Net Carbs 2g

Cauliflower Cheese Dip

Preparation Time: 5 Minutes

Cooking Time: 15 Minutes

Servings: 6

Ingredients:

- One small head cauliflower, chopped
- ¾ cup chicken broth
- ¼ teaspoon ground cumin
- ¼ teaspoon chili powder
- ¼ teaspoon garlic powder
- Salt and pepper to taste
- 1/3 cup cream cheese, chopped
- Two tablespoons canned coconut milk

Directions:

1. Combine the cauliflower and chicken broth in a saucepan and simmer until the cauliflower is tender.
2. Add the cumin, chili powder, and garlic powder, then season with salt and pepper.
3. Stir in the cream cheese until melted, then blend everything with an immersion blender.
4. Whisk in the coconut milk, then spoon into a serving bowl.

5. Serve with sliced celery sticks.

Nutrition: Calories 75 Fat 6g Protein 2.5g Net Carbs 2g

Deviled Eggs with Bacon

Preparation Time: 2 Minutes

Cooking Time: 20 Minutes

Servings: 6

Ingredients:

- Six large eggs
- Three slices of thick-cut bacon
- ¼ cup avocado oil mayonnaise
- 1 teaspoon Dijon mustard

Directions:

1. Place the eggs in a saucepan, then pour it with water.
2. Bring the water to boil, then remove from heat and let rest for 10 minutes.
3. Meanwhile, cook the bacon in a skillet over medium-high heat until crisp.
4. Rinse the eggs in cold water until cool enough to handle, then peel them.
5. Cut the eggs in half and spoon the yolks into a bowl.
6. Add one tablespoon of bacon fat from the skillet along with the mayonnaise and mustard.
7. Spoon the mixture into the egg halves, then crumble the bacon over the top.

Nutrition: Calories 145 Fat 11g Protein 8.5g Net Carbs 3g

CPSIA information can be obtained
at www.ICGtesting.com
Printed in the USA
BVHW041517190321
602997BV00010B/605